EMMANUEL JOSEPH

Pillars of Life, How Mythology Informs the Architecture of Health and Healing

Copyright © 2025 by Emmanuel Joseph

All rights reserved. No part of this publication may be reproduced, stored or transmitted in any form or by any means, electronic, mechanical, photocopying, recording, scanning, or otherwise without written permission from the publisher. It is illegal to copy this book, post it to a website, or distribute it by any other means without permission.

First edition

This book was professionally typeset on Reedsy.
Find out more at reedsy.com

Contents

1. Chapter 1: The Foundation of Myths and Health — 1
2. Chapter 2: The Myth of Asclepius and the Art of Healing — 3
3. Chapter 3: The Egyptian Imhotep and the Birth of Medicine — 5
4. Chapter 4: Hindu Mythology and the Balance of Life Energies — 7
5. Chapter 5: Norse Mythology and the Resilience of the Human... — 9
6. Chapter 6: Chinese Mythology and the Harmony of Yin and Yang — 11
7. Chapter 7: Native American Mythology and the Power of Nature — 13
8. Chapter 8: The Celtic Cailleach and Seasonal Healing — 15
9. Chapter 9: The Japanese Shinto Kami and Spiritual Wellness — 17
10. Chapter 10: African Mythology and the Wisdom of the... — 19
11. Chapter 11: The Incan Pachamama and Earthly Nourishment — 21
12. Chapter 12: The Modern Relevance of Mythology in Health — 23
13. Chapter 13: Aboriginal Dreamtime and the Spiritual Landscape... — 25
14. Chapter 14: Hawaiian Mythology and the Healing Power of Mana — 27
15. Chapter 15: The Mythological Synthesis and Future of Health — 29

1

Chapter 1: The Foundation of Myths and Health

Mythology often serves as a mirror reflecting the collective consciousness of a society. Many ancient cultures relied on these stories to explain natural phenomena, including health and illness. For example, in Greek mythology, the god Asclepius was revered as a healer, symbolizing the ancient Greeks' understanding of medicine and wellness. These myths provided a framework for early medical practices, merging spiritual beliefs with physical treatments.

In many indigenous cultures, shamans and healers used mythological narratives to guide their healing practices. These stories were not merely tales but were integral to the rituals and ceremonies that promoted health. By invoking the spirits or gods associated with healing, these practitioners aimed to restore balance within the individual and the community. This holistic approach to health, deeply rooted in mythology, continues to influence modern alternative medicine.

The concept of health in ancient myths often extends beyond the physical body to encompass the mind and spirit. For instance, in Hindu mythology, the balance of the body's energies, or chakras, is crucial for overall well-being. This idea has found its way into contemporary wellness practices, such as yoga and meditation, which emphasize the interconnectedness of the body and mind. Thus, mythology provides a multidimensional perspective on health that remains relevant today.

By understanding the mythological underpinnings of health practices, we can appreciate the depth and richness of ancient wisdom. These stories, though often fantastical, offer profound insights into the human condition and the eternal quest for healing. As we delve deeper into the myths, we uncover the timeless principles that continue to guide our journey toward health and wellness.

2

Chapter 2: The Myth of Asclepius and the Art of Healing

Asclepius, the Greek god of medicine, stands as a testament to the ancient Greeks' reverence for the healing arts. Born to the god Apollo and the mortal woman Coronis, Asclepius was endowed with divine knowledge of medicine. His story illustrates the Greeks' understanding of the delicate balance between life and death and the healer's role in navigating this balance.

According to myth, Asclepius was taught the art of healing by the centaur Chiron, a wise and skilled teacher. Chiron's tutelage symbolizes the transmission of medical knowledge from one generation to the next. This mentorship model persists in modern medical education, where experienced practitioners guide and train the next wave of healers.

Asclepius's healing abilities were so profound that he could even resurrect the dead, a feat that angered Zeus, the king of the gods. Fearing that humans would become immortal, Zeus struck Asclepius down with a thunderbolt. This story underscores the limitations and ethical dilemmas faced by healers, a theme that resonates in contemporary medical practice. The balance between extending life and respecting the natural course of death remains a crucial consideration in healthcare.

Temples dedicated to Asclepius, known as Asclepieia, served as healing centers where patients sought cures for their ailments. These temples were precursors to modern hospitals, providing a sanctuary for the sick and a space for holistic healing. By studying these ancient practices, we gain a deeper appreciation for the evolution of healthcare and the enduring legacy of mythological influences.

3

Chapter 3: The Egyptian Imhotep and the Birth of Medicine

In ancient Egypt, the figure of Imhotep holds a significant place in the annals of medical history. Renowned as a polymath, Imhotep was a high priest, architect, and physician who served under Pharaoh Djoser. His contributions to medicine were so impactful that he was later deified and worshipped as a god of healing.

Imhotep's role as a healer is immortalized in various Egyptian myths and texts. He is credited with the creation of the Edwin Smith Papyrus, one of the oldest known medical treatises. This document, which outlines surgical procedures and treatments, exemplifies the advanced state of Egyptian medicine. The reverence for Imhotep's knowledge and skill highlights the importance of empirical observation and documentation in medical practice.

The worship of Imhotep extended beyond his lifetime, with temples and shrines dedicated to his cult. Pilgrims would visit these sites seeking cures for their ailments, much like the Asclepieia of ancient Greece. This practice underscores the intersection of spirituality and medicine, where divine intervention and practical treatments coexisted. The legacy of Imhotep continues to inspire modern medicine, emphasizing the importance of holistic and integrative approaches to health.

Imhotep's mythological status as a god of healing reflects the ancient

Egyptians' deep respect for medical knowledge and innovation. His story serves as a reminder of the timeless quest for understanding the human body and the relentless pursuit of healing. By exploring Imhotep's contributions, we gain insight into the foundational principles of medicine that continue to inform contemporary practices.

4

Chapter 4: Hindu Mythology and the Balance of Life Energies

Hindu mythology presents a rich tapestry of stories that emphasize the balance of life energies, or prana, as essential for health and healing. Central to this belief is the concept of chakras, the energy centers within the body that regulate physical, mental, and spiritual well-being. The alignment and balance of these chakras are crucial for maintaining harmony and preventing illness.

The mythology surrounding Lord Shiva, one of the principal deities in Hinduism, illustrates the importance of meditation and inner balance. Shiva, often depicted in deep meditation, embodies the ideal of self-control and mastery over the body's energies. This focus on meditation and mindfulness has permeated modern wellness practices, highlighting the interconnectedness of the mind and body.

The Ayurvedic system of medicine, rooted in Hindu mythology, emphasizes the balance of the three doshas: Vata, Pitta, and Kapha. These doshas represent different bodily energies, and their harmony is essential for health. The ancient texts of Ayurveda provide a comprehensive framework for understanding the body's constitution and offer remedies to restore balance. This holistic approach, steeped in mythology, continues to influence contemporary integrative medicine.

Mythological stories in Hinduism also highlight the role of divine intervention in healing. The tale of Dhanvantari, the god of Ayurveda, underscores the belief in divine wisdom guiding medical practices. Dhanvantari's emergence from the churning of the ocean symbolizes the quest for immortality and the discovery of the elixir of life. This myth serves as a metaphor for the continuous pursuit of knowledge and the search for cures in the field of medicine.

5

Chapter 5: Norse Mythology and the Resilience of the Human Spirit

Norse mythology, with its tales of gods, giants, and heroic deeds, offers profound insights into the resilience of the human spirit and the quest for healing. The myths emphasize the themes of strength, endurance, and the eternal struggle against adversity, which resonate with the principles of health and well-being.

One of the most significant figures in Norse mythology is Eir, the goddess of healing. Eir's association with healing herbs and medicinal knowledge highlights the importance of natural remedies and the connection between humans and nature. Her role as a healer reflects the ancient Norse understanding of health, where the natural environment played a crucial role in maintaining well-being.

The myths surrounding the god Odin, who sacrificed his eye for wisdom, illustrate the value placed on knowledge and the lengths to which one might go to obtain it. Odin's pursuit of wisdom is akin to the modern quest for medical breakthroughs and understanding. This relentless search for knowledge and the willingness to make sacrifices for the greater good are central to the ethos of healthcare and scientific research.

The resilience of the human spirit is a recurring theme in Norse mythology, as evidenced by the tale of Baldr's resurrection. Baldr, a beloved god, is killed, but his return to life symbolizes hope and renewal. This story serves as a metaphor for the healing process, where recovery and rejuvenation are possible despite life's challenges. The themes of resilience and hope in Norse mythology continue to inspire contemporary approaches to mental health and recovery.

6

Chapter 6: Chinese Mythology and the Harmony of Yin and Yang

Chinese mythology, deeply intertwined with philosophical concepts, provides a unique perspective on health and healing through the principles of Yin and Yang. These dual forces represent the balance of opposites, which is essential for maintaining harmony within the body and the universe.

The mythological figure of Shennong, the Divine Farmer, is revered as the father of Chinese medicine. According to legend, Shennong tasted hundreds of herbs to understand their medicinal properties and compiled his knowledge in the Shennong Bencao Jing, an ancient pharmacopoeia. This myth underscores the importance of empirical observation and experimentation in the development of medical knowledge.

The concept of Qi, or life force, is central to Chinese mythology and traditional Chinese medicine (TCM). Qi flows through the body's meridians, and its balance is crucial for health. The myths surrounding the Yellow Emperor, Huangdi, highlight the significance of Qi and the techniques used to regulate its flow, such as acupuncture and herbal medicine. These ancient practices continue to be integral to TCM and have gained recognition in Western medicine for their holistic approach to health.

The interplay of Yin and Yang is also evident in the myth of Nuwa and

Fuxi, who are credited with creating humanity and teaching essential skills. Their harmonious relationship symbolizes the balance that is necessary for a healthy and prosperous life. This principle of balance extends to various aspects of health, from diet and exercise to emotional and mental well-being. The enduring legacy of Yin and Yang in Chinese mythology offers valuable insights into the interconnectedness of all elements of life and the importance of maintaining equilibrium.

7

Chapter 7: Native American Mythology and the Power of Nature

Native American mythology is deeply rooted in the natural world, reflecting a profound respect for nature's healing powers. Many tribes have myths and legends that emphasize the interconnectedness of all living things and the importance of harmony with the environment. These stories often highlight the role of animals, plants, and natural elements in promoting health and well-being.

The myth of the Great Spirit, a central figure in many Native American cultures, underscores the belief in a higher power that oversees the balance of life. This spiritual force is thought to guide and protect individuals, providing strength and healing. The reverence for the Great Spirit reflects the holistic approach to health, where physical, mental, and spiritual well-being are interconnected.

Healing ceremonies and rituals are integral to Native American mythology, often involving chants, dances, and the use of medicinal herbs. The story of the White Buffalo Calf Woman, a sacred figure among the Lakota people, illustrates the significance of these practices. She is said to have brought the sacred pipe, which is used in ceremonies to promote peace, healing, and spiritual connection. These rituals emphasize the importance of community and the collective effort to restore balance and harmony.

Native American myths also highlight the healing power of nature, with many stories involving medicinal plants and animals. The tale of the Healing Bear, for example, depicts a bear that teaches humans about the healing properties of herbs and roots. This myth reflects the deep knowledge of natural remedies that Native Americans possess and their enduring legacy in modern herbal medicine.

8

Chapter 8: The Celtic Cailleach and Seasonal Healing

Celtic mythology, rich with stories of gods, goddesses, and supernatural beings, offers a unique perspective on health and healing through the lens of nature and the changing seasons. One of the most intriguing figures in Celtic mythology is the Cailleach, an ancient goddess associated with winter and the natural cycles of life and death.

The Cailleach, often depicted as an old woman, symbolizes the wisdom and transformative power of nature. Her role in Celtic mythology highlights the importance of the seasons and their influence on health and well-being. The Cailleach's ability to control the weather and bring about winter underscores the idea that health is closely linked to the natural world and its cycles.

The myth of the Cailleach emphasizes the need for adaptation and resilience in the face of changing conditions. Just as the seasons shift from winter to spring, individuals must navigate the challenges of life and health. The story of the Cailleach teaches the importance of patience, perseverance, and the acceptance of natural cycles as essential elements of healing.

Celtic healing practices often involved rituals and ceremonies that honored the natural world and its cycles. The use of sacred wells, healing herbs, and seasonal festivals underscores the connection between health and nature. The Beltane festival, for example, celebrated the arrival of spring and the renewal of life, symbolizing the importance of seasonal transitions in maintaining health and well-being.

9

Chapter 9: The Japanese Shinto Kami and Spiritual Wellness

Shinto, the indigenous religion of Japan, is deeply intertwined with Japanese mythology and emphasizes the worship of kami, or spirits, that inhabit natural objects and phenomena. These kami play a significant role in promoting health and healing, reflecting the Shinto belief in the interconnectedness of the spiritual and physical worlds.

The myth of Amaterasu, the sun goddess and one of the most important kami, illustrates the connection between light, life, and health. Amaterasu's retreat into a cave, plunging the world into darkness, symbolizes the impact of spiritual imbalance on physical well-being. Her eventual return, bringing light and warmth back to the world, highlights the importance of restoring harmony and balance for health.

Shinto rituals and practices often involve purification and offerings to the kami, seeking their blessings for health and protection. The concept of harae, or purification, is central to Shinto and reflects the belief that physical and spiritual cleansing is essential for well-being. This practice underscores the importance of maintaining a harmonious relationship with the spiritual world to promote health.

Sacred sites, such as shrines and natural landmarks, are integral to Shinto healing practices. The Ise Grand Shrine, dedicated to Amaterasu, is a place of pilgrimage and spiritual renewal. These sacred spaces provide a sanctuary for individuals to connect with the kami and seek their healing influence. The reverence for nature and the belief in the healing power of the kami continue to inspire modern spiritual practices and holistic approaches to health.

10

Chapter 10: African Mythology and the Wisdom of the Ancestors

African mythology, with its rich tapestry of stories and legends, offers profound insights into health and healing through the wisdom of the ancestors and the natural world. Many African cultures believe in the presence of ancestral spirits who guide and protect the living, playing a crucial role in promoting health and well-being.

The myth of the Yoruba deity Osanyin, the god of herbal medicine, highlights the importance of natural remedies and the deep knowledge of medicinal plants. Osanyin is believed to possess the wisdom of all herbs and their healing properties, reflecting the Yoruba understanding of the connection between nature and health. This emphasis on herbal medicine continues to influence traditional healing practices in Africa.

Ancestor worship is a central theme in African mythology, underscoring the belief that the spirits of the departed continue to play an active role in the lives of the living. The ancestors are revered as sources of wisdom and guidance, and their blessings are sought for health and protection. This practice highlights the importance of maintaining a strong connection with one's heritage and the collective knowledge of the community.

Healing ceremonies and rituals are integral to African mythology, often involving music, dance, and the use of sacred objects. The story of the Zulu healer Mbokodo, who received his healing powers from the ancestors, illustrates the significance of these practices. Mbokodo's ability to communicate with the ancestral spirits and use their guidance for healing reflects the holistic approach to health that is deeply rooted in African culture.

11

Chapter 11: The Incan Pachamama and Earthly Nourishment

Incan mythology, with its reverence for nature and the cosmos, offers valuable insights into the relationship between health and the natural world. Pachamama, the Earth Mother, is a central figure in Incan beliefs, symbolizing fertility, nourishment, and the interconnectedness of all life.

Pachamama is revered as the provider of life-sustaining resources, such as food and water. The myths surrounding her emphasize the importance of maintaining a harmonious relationship with the earth to ensure health and well-being. This connection between environmental stewardship and health is reflected in modern sustainable practices that promote the well-being of both the planet and its inhabitants.

Incan rituals and ceremonies often involved offerings to Pachamama, seeking her blessings for a bountiful harvest and protection from natural disasters. These practices highlight the belief that the health of the individual and the community is closely linked to the health of the environment. The reverence for Pachamama underscores the importance of living in harmony with nature and recognizing the interdependence of all life forms.

The Incan concept of ayni, or reciprocity, further illustrates the interconnectedness of health and nature. Ayni involves the exchange of energy and resources between individuals, communities, and the natural world, promoting balance and harmony. This principle reflects the holistic approach to health that is central to Incan mythology and continues to inspire contemporary sustainable practices.

12

Chapter 12: The Modern Relevance of Mythology in Health

As we navigate the complexities of modern life, the timeless wisdom of mythology continues to inform our understanding of health and healing. By examining the myths and legends of different cultures, we gain valuable insights into the principles that underpin holistic well-being.

Mythology offers a multidimensional perspective on health, emphasizing the interconnectedness of the physical, mental, and spiritual aspects of well-being. The stories of gods, goddesses, and supernatural beings provide a rich tapestry of knowledge that transcends time and space, offering guidance and inspiration for contemporary health practices.

The holistic approach to health, deeply rooted in mythology, underscores the importance of balance and harmony. Whether through the balance of energies, the connection with nature, or the wisdom of the ancestors, these ancient stories remind us of the fundamental principles that promote well-being. By integrating these principles into modern medicine and wellness practices, we can create a more comprehensive and integrative approach to health.

In conclusion, mythology serves as a powerful tool for understanding the complexities of health and healing. The stories and legends of ancient cultures offer timeless insights that continue to resonate in our quest for well-being.

By embracing the wisdom of mythology, we can enrich our approach to health and create a more harmonious and balanced world.

13

Chapter 13: Aboriginal Dreamtime and the Spiritual Landscape of Health

Aboriginal Dreamtime stories, or Dreamings, are central to the spiritual and cultural identity of Indigenous Australians. These myths convey the creation of the world and the origins of life, deeply influencing the Aboriginal understanding of health and healing. Dreamtime stories emphasize the interconnectedness of the land, people, and the spirit world, offering a holistic perspective on well-being.

The myth of the Rainbow Serpent, a powerful creation figure, illustrates the significance of water and the natural environment in maintaining health. The Rainbow Serpent is believed to have shaped the landscape, creating rivers, mountains, and valleys. This story underscores the importance of respecting and preserving the natural world, as it is intrinsically linked to the health and survival of the community.

Healing practices in Aboriginal culture often involve rituals and ceremonies that connect individuals to their ancestral spirits and the land. The use of traditional medicines, derived from native plants, reflects the deep knowledge of the natural world possessed by Aboriginal healers. These practices highlight the importance of harmony with nature and the spiritual dimensions of health, which continue to inspire contemporary approaches to holistic healing.

Dreamtime stories also emphasize the role of community in promoting health and well-being. The collective nature of these myths reinforces the idea that health is a shared responsibility, requiring the support and cooperation of the entire community. This sense of interconnectedness and mutual support remains a vital aspect of Aboriginal health practices and offers valuable lessons for modern healthcare systems.

14

Chapter 14: Hawaiian Mythology and the Healing Power of Mana

Hawaiian mythology, with its rich tapestry of gods, goddesses, and supernatural beings, provides a unique perspective on health and healing through the concept of mana. Mana is a spiritual energy or life force that flows through all living things, and its balance is essential for maintaining health and well-being.

The myth of Pele, the volcano goddess, illustrates the dynamic and transformative power of mana. Pele's fiery presence and volcanic activity symbolize the creation and destruction inherent in the natural world. This myth highlights the importance of recognizing and harnessing the powerful energies within and around us to promote healing and renewal.

Hawaiian healing practices often involve the use of natural remedies, such as medicinal plants and lomilomi massage, to restore the balance of mana within the body. The story of Kamapua'a, the pig god associated with agriculture and fertility, underscores the significance of the natural world in providing the resources necessary for health. These practices emphasize the importance of living in harmony with nature and maintaining the flow of mana to support well-being.

Rituals and ceremonies, such as the hula dance, play a crucial role in Hawaiian healing practices. The hula, accompanied by chants and music, is a form of storytelling that connects individuals to their ancestors and the spiritual world. This cultural expression of mana through dance and song highlights the interconnectedness of the physical, mental, and spiritual aspects of health, offering valuable insights into the holistic approach to healing.

15

Chapter 15: The Mythological Synthesis and Future of Health

As we explore the diverse mythologies of different cultures, a common thread emerges: the belief in the interconnectedness of all aspects of life and the importance of balance and harmony for health and well-being. These ancient stories provide a rich source of wisdom that continues to inform and inspire contemporary approaches to health and healing.

The synthesis of mythological concepts and modern medicine offers a holistic framework for understanding health. By integrating the spiritual, mental, and physical dimensions of well-being, we can create more comprehensive and effective healthcare practices. This holistic approach emphasizes the importance of preventive care, mindfulness, and the nurturing of our connection to nature and community.

The future of health and healing lies in the ability to draw on the timeless wisdom of mythology while embracing the advancements of modern science. Innovations in medical technology and research can be enriched by the principles and practices rooted in ancient myths. This fusion of old and new offers a path toward a more balanced and integrative approach to health.

In conclusion, the exploration of mythology reveals the enduring relevance of these ancient stories in shaping our understanding of health and healing. By honoring the wisdom of the past and embracing the possibilities of the future, we can build a more harmonious and holistic approach to well-being. The pillars of life, as illuminated by mythology, continue to guide us on our journey toward health and healing.

Pillars of Life: How Mythology Informs the Architecture of Health and Healing

explores the timeless wisdom found within mythological stories and their influence on modern health practices. This book takes you on a journey through various cultures and eras, uncovering how ancient legends shape our views on physical, mental, and spiritual well-being. From the Greek god of medicine, Asclepius, to the Japanese kami, each chapter presents unique insights into the interconnectedness of health and mythology. This book is an engaging exploration of how myths continue to inform and inspire our pursuit of holistic wellness today.

www.ingramcontent.com/pod-product-compliance
Lightning Source LLC
LaVergne TN
LVHW020502080526
838202LV00057B/6110